BRITAIN'S
COLD WAR

First published 2014

Amberley Publishing
The Hill, Stroud, Gloucestershire, GL5 4EP
www.amberley-books.com

ISBN 978 1 4456 3998 7 (print)
ISBN 978 1 4456 4009 9(ebook)

British Library Cataloguing in Publication Data.
A catalogue record for this book is available from the British Library.

Typesetting by Amberley Publishing.
Printed in Great Britain.

BRITAIN'S COLD WAR

THE DANGEROUS DECADES

An Illustrated History

BOB CLARKE

AMBERLEY

Contents

Acknowledgements

Books such as this are not possible without the skill of the photographer – I would like to extend my gratitude to those who risk their lives in the field. As for the text, I must thank Peter and Debra Melsom, and Emma Elton, for taking the time to read over the proofs and make suggestions. Any errors are, naturally, my own.

Introduction

The Cold War is different to many other events of the twentieth century, especially in its longevity. Indeed, research I have recently carried out with the University of Exeter suggests that the period is so long it really shouldn't be classed as an entity at all. The name encapsulates an almost bewildering range of events – nowhere more so than in the United Kingdom. To my mind, we need to consider more than just the traditionally recognisable aspects of the Cold War if we are to understand its wide-ranging effects.

So, rather than investigating the development of weapons systems or depicting one or other nuclear tests, this series of images is intended to remind us of all those activities on the edge of the mainstream events. The effects, especially socially, were surprisingly far reaching, so much so the period is unrecognisable to those who did not experience it. What we present here appears, on the face of it, to be a somewhat eclectic mix of images. On closer inspection, I hope you will realise they actually all depict facets of the Cold War from the British perspective. Some will be recognisable, other less so, but they all do have something in common, they are all part of the rich tapestry of British life from the perspective of the Cold War.

Utilising a range of images, I hope I have portrayed something of the Cold War from a more public-orientated direction. The chapters are arranged decade by decade, allowing the reader to appreciate the length of time for which some aspects bubbled along just under the surface of everyday life. I also included the many voluntary organisations that were so much a part of many lives, sometimes for the entire Cold War period. There is also mention of the numerous military actions the United Kingdom was involved in around the world and on the home front.

The images utilised here come from a wide range of sources. Where possible they relay a specific event or activity, but when talking about some sites (particularly military areas) a more modern image is used, demonstrating that the archaeology of the Cold War is all around us and will continue to be so for a long time yet.

Bob Clarke
2014

1940s

Redrawing the Political Map of Europe

By the end of 1945, over 56 million lay dead (the effects of global total war), much of Europe and Eastern Asia was in ruins and political unrest was everywhere. In Britain, Churchill had been replaced by Clement Attlee in a surprise election victory for the Labour Party, and Harry Truman had taken over the Presidency of the United States on the death of Theodore Roosevelt. Only Stalin remained. In his now famous speech at Fulton, Missouri, on 5 March 1946, Churchill summed the situation up:

> From Stettin in the Baltic to Trieste in the Adriatic an iron curtain has descended across the Continent. Behind that line lie all the capitals of the ancient states of Central and Eastern Europe. Warsaw, Berlin, Prague, Vienna, Budapest, Bucharest and Sofia; all these famous cities and the populations around them lie in what I must call the Soviet sphere, and all are subject, in one form or another, not only to Soviet influence but to a very high and in some cases increasing measure of control from Moscow.
>
> Winston Churchill, 5 March 1946

Many thought Churchill, now out of office, was sensationalising the situation, but by 1948 it was clear he was not. This decade saw British troops in action against communist uprisings around the world, while supporting what would now be classed as 'humanitarian aid' in Europe. This decade ushered in the nuclear age, changing the face of warfare forever, forcing Britain to readopt a warlike footing; rearming and mobilising thousands in the name of civil defence. By the time the decade was out, the Cold War was well and truly underway.

1945 – The End of the Reich: British and Soviet Troops Meet at Wismar on 3 May.

Just six days after this photograph was taken, the war in Europe was over. The Allies, so intent on destroying the Nazi regime, had, in the process, completely devastated most of Germany. Indeed, six years of total war had reduced large parts of Europe's infrastructure to rubble. It was this landscape the Allies now inherited. It was also a landscape in which Stalin saw potential.

ROYAL OBSERVER CORPS.

PHOTO MASSERS. MALTON.

H4 Post, Sherburn, Yorks.   June, 1945

1945 – Royal Observer Corps Stand Down, Sherburn, North Yorkshire

While millions of Britons were in uniformed service across the world, millions more were supporting the war effort through membership of voluntary services on the home front. This included the Civil Defence, Auxiliary Fire Service and Royal Observer Corps (ROC). All three organisations were to be resurrected in the face of growing Soviet belligerence just a few years later. The ROC began offering terms of service to original members in November 1946, and training restarted on 1 January 1947. However, in those few years of stand-down, the world had changed forever. Atomic warfare now seemed likely. (*Picture courtesy John Clarke Collection*)

58381 A.C.

9 August 1945 – Nagasaki: The Second Nuclear Detonation Over Japan

Just three days after the first offensive detonation of a nuclear weapon, the second was deployed over Nagasaki. The airburst weapon, an implosion device, exploded around 1,600 feet above the city; nearly 90,000 died on the day or afterwards due to burns and radiation. British nuclear scientist William Penney and Group Captain Leonard Cheshire were observers on the day. Penney was to head up the development of Britain's own nuclear capability.

1946 – Greek Civil War

The power vacuum left by the retreating Italian and German armies was soon contested by returning government and communist forces. After months of unrest, the situation spilled out into open civil war. By 1947, the British government, who had been supporting Greek government forces with financial and military aid, could no longer afford the outlay and had to ask the United States for help. It came in the form of the Truman Doctrine, an aggressive, economic policy through which the United States would guarantee, where possible, any force opposing communist rule. The Greek Civil War is widely recognised as the first conflict of the Cold War.

Above: 1947 – Authorisation for the British Bomb

In early January 1947, the British government finally authorised a team led by William (later Lord) Penney to develop a purely British nuclear device. This had been forced by the McMahon Act of August 1946, which effectively halted all information exchanges between the United States and any other country. It would be five years before the team had produced a viable device. William Penney is shown on the left, with John Cockroft on the right.

Opposite above: 22 July 1946 – King David Hotel Bombing, Jerusalem

British civil administration in Palestine (formed in 1920) had promised to support the formation of a Jewish nation in the region. After the Second World War, the United Nations suggested the area be partitioned, forming two separate states. Britain accepted the proposal in principle, but would not outwardly support it for fear of losing influence with Arab states in the region. The southern wing of the King David Hotel housed the central offices of the British Mandate of Palestine. The bombing was carried out by the Irgun, a right-wing Zionist organisation, in response to Operation Agatha, a wide range of raids on 'illegal' organisations carried out by the British authorities across the Mandatory. It was the deadliest attack of the whole of the British Mandate, killing ninety-one people. (*Image courtesy National Library of Israel*)

Opposite below: 1946 – British soldiers in Tel Aviv Enforcing a Curfew After Terrorist Attacks in the Region

After the bombing of the King David Hotel, British forces clamped down on Jewish organisations, but both Arab and Jewish administrations were, by now, unhappy with the British Mandate. As the Mandate expired in May 1948, the arguments between Arabs and Jews transitioned from civil to nation state warfare. The situation continues to dominate Middle Eastern politics to this day, due in part to the failings of British foreign policy. (*Picture courtesy Haim Fain, National Library of Israel*)

Above: 1948 – Berlin Sectors

At the end of the Second World War, Germany was divided into four zones; initially purely administrative but increasingly politically charged as the decade played out. These were run by the Allies. Berlin, which lay deep inside the Soviet Zone, was divided into four sectors, again split between the four victors. This divided country was a ripe breeding ground for communism and, by the end of the year, Berlin was to be the cause of the first major face-off between East and West as Stalin tried to force the Western Allies from Berlin.

Opposite page: **April 1948 – Recipient Countries of American Economic Aid (Marshall Plan)**

The European Recovery Programme, known as the Marshall Plan after Gen. (ret.) George Marshall, President Truman's Secretary of State, was the United States' attempt to reduce the effects and spread of communism. An important component of Truman's anti-Soviet doctrine, the plan offered economic aid to all former allies of the United States; unsurprisingly, the Soviet Union and those countries now behind the 'Iron Curtain' refused.

1948 – Postal Label for Aid Travelling to Europe (Marshall Plan)

During the four years the Marshall Plan was in operation, over US$16 billion in economic aid, technical advice and materials was donated to Europe. Of the seventeen countries who asked for aid, the United Kingdom received by far the most help – US$3,297 million in all – not all in cash; over 500 TO-20 Grey Ferguson tractors were constructed by the manufacturer in Detroit and imported to Britain. The American public were also encouraged to send aid, attracting reduced postage naturally.

2 April 1948 – The 'Little Lift'

After a protracted period arguing about currency change and political ownership of parts of Germany, the Soviet occupying forces closed off land routes to Berlin. Using mainly C-47s, the Royal Air Force and aircraft from the United States managed to supply the sector garrisons in Berlin via an airfreight bridge. By the end of April, the majority of restrictions had been lifted, but Stalin now knew he could cause major disruption for the Allies almost overnight.

5 April 1948 – British European Airways Vickers Viking

The Little Lift proved that it would, for short periods at least, be possible to deliver essential supplies by air, although it was not without its hazards. On 5 April, a Viking operated by BEA on a scheduled flight into Berlin was buzzed by a Soviet Yak-3. On final approach into Gatow, an airfield in the British Sector, the Yak-3 attempted a further close fly-by, misjudged the manoeuvre and hit the Viking head on. All fourteen passengers in the Viking died, as did the Soviet pilot. This unfortunate event made the Soviets more wary of interfering with air traffic, and also strengthened the resolve of the Western Allies to use air freight if needed.

24 June 1948 – Berlin Blockade, Unloading Supplies at Gatow

Tensions over the April restrictions continued to have an effect on the way Berlin was administered. On 24 June, while the Western Allies were introducing a new currency in their zones, the Soviet authorities suspended all freight traffic between East and West. Road, rail and water traffic was to be non-existent until May 1949. The only way to support 2 million people now blockaded in Berlin was by air. (*Courtesy Frank Watt*)

17 July 1948 – The 'Atomic' Bombers Arrive in Britain

It was clear by the middle of July that the Soviets intended to maintain their stranglehold on Berlin. British Foreign Secretary Ernest Bevin was convinced that the Soviets needed a show of strength, not diplomacy, if the siege was to be broken. Accordingly, on 17 July 1948, the first squadrons of what the press called 'The "Atomic" Bombers' landed at RAF Scampton. Over sixty years later, nuclear-capable aircraft from the United States are still stationed here.

1948 – American Servicemen 'Back Over Here'. Airman Second Class, Guy Kenney, visits Blackpool

Accompanying the first wave of 'Atomic' B-29s were over 1,500 servicemen, mostly stationed at one station near Warrington – RAF Burtonwood. Burtonwood would become a major servicing depot, eventually supporting the vast fleet of C-54 transport aircraft that were operating on the airlift. It also signalled the return of American servicemen and their effects on the British way of life. Britain is still a major posting for the United States. (*Courtesy Guy Kenney*)

18 October 1948 – Malaya RAF Ground Crew Rearming a Bristol Beaufighter

The aircraft proved to be very effective in the COIN (Counter Insurgency) role. After a protracted period of civil unrest, primarily caused by the collapse of Japan in 1945, the Malayan Communist Party (MCP) began offensive activities. Three European plantation managers were murdered on 16 June 1948, and by July British troops were enforcing emergency measures across the country. Anyone suspected of being a communist was imprisoned without trial under the new legislation. The MCP formed a subsidiary movement, The Malayan People's Liberation Army (MPLA), a guerrilla organisation that targeted a number of economic centres.

1948 – Two Men of the Malay Regiment Locating the Position of Bandit Hideouts on the Map, Malaya

Within a year, a substantial force of Commonwealth troops was complementing a large police force. This included 22,000 special constables, who had been recruited by plantation and mine managers, all employed on anti-terrorist duties. During the campaign, Britain used defoliation chemicals in an attempt to deny some of the dense forest cover. This and many other activities, such as 'resettlement' programmes and saturation bombing were later utilised by the United States in Vietnam, who cited their use in Malaya as a basis for legality. The insurgency was finally defeated in 1960.

1948 – Merry Christmas from the Airlift

The airlift had a major affect on British service personnel. Thousands who were about to be demobbed had their terms of service extended, and over 100 ageing C-47s were pressed back into service. The airlift soon spawned its own industry, with souvenirs manufactured in Germany making their way to the United Kingdom. There was also a brisk trade in watches and cameras, with many being traded for coffee and flown back in RAF aircraft returning to the UK for servicing. (*Courtesy Frank Watt*)

SURREY DIVISION

HEADQUARTERS
WARDENS
RESCUE
AMBULANCE
WELFARE

CIVIL DEFENCE NEEDS YOU NOW!

TO OBTAIN FULL PARTICULARS OF YOUR LOCAL CIVIL DEFENCE UNIT—

P.T.O.

1949 – Civil Defence Corps

In 1948, in direct response to events in Berlin, the Civil Defence Act passed through Parliament. Local authorities were now required, by law, to prepare for the protection of the public by organising services capable of supporting them in a national emergency. This included the raising and training of the Civil Defence Corps. Training started in January 1949 and was initially organised along similar lines to the civil defence effort in the Second World War.

1948 – Auxiliary Fire Service

The Auxiliary Fire Service (AFS) had, until 1941, supported the local authorities' fire brigade, and for the duration of the war both entities were subsumed into the National Fire Service. In 1948, the service was redistributed to the local authorities and the AFS was stood down. By November that year, the AFS was back in business, required by the Civil Defence Act 1948. Initially equipped with war surplus pumps, the AFS was to become linked with one of the Cold War's most iconic vehicles – the Green Goddess.

1949 – The RAF Delivers the Millionth Ton of Supplies

On 18 February 1949, a York aircraft took off from RAF Wunstorf bound for RAF Gatow. It carried an eclectic mix of supplies, including raisins, meat, potatoes, butter and hay. More importantly, the load contained the millionth ton to be delivered by air into the city. This achievement was made all the more remarkable given that no aircraft at the time was capable of carrying more than 10 tons!

1949 – North Atlantic Treaty Organisation, Signing the Agreement, 4 April

On 4 April 1949, eleven European countries, along with the United States, signed the North Atlantic Treaty in Washington D.C. The first Secretary General of the organisation was Lord Ismay who, when discussing the role of NATO, described it as keeping 'the Russians out, the Americans in and the Germans down'. In truth, NATO had two primary aims: to present a united European military front in the face of Soviet policy; and to reduce the possibility of independent nation state foreign policy in Europe ever developing again.

12 May 1949 – The End of the Blockade, but Not the Airlift

Soviet restrictions to land and water traffic were lifted on 12 May 1949, although the supply of Berlin from the air would never really stop until unification on 3 October 1990. The airlift delivered 2,326,406 tons, 68 per cent of which was coal, on 278,228 flights. In doing so, it placed Berlin firmly at the centre of much of the later Cold War politics.

1 October 1949 – Mao Tse-tung Forms the People's Republic of China

For two decades, the Chinese communists struggled with the Kuomintang Party for control of the country. In 1947, the situation suddenly swung in the communists' favour and, on 1 October 1949, after a number of audacious battles, the communists, led by Mao Tse-tung, announced the formation of the People's Republic of China. Stalin was surprised at the communist victory, and was also more than a little concerned, as this was a different interpretation of the words of Marx. More importantly, Moscow had no hand in creating the new communist state, and subsequent relations between the two giant neighbouring states were rocky throughout the Cold War.

Opposite page: 1949 – 'The Atomic Cities', Civil Defence Corps Training at Easingwold, North Yorkshire

While the local authorities were responsible for recruitment, central government undertook the training of instructors at a national level. Three schools were reopened, having previously been used throughout the Second World War, and were equipped with specialist training grounds. These became known as the 'Atomic Cities'. Streets of partially bombed out houses were constructed, along with other hazardous situations, at Falfield in Gloucestershire. There was even a derailed train. Instructors who graduated at the centres then went on to train the local volunteers at county-run facilities.

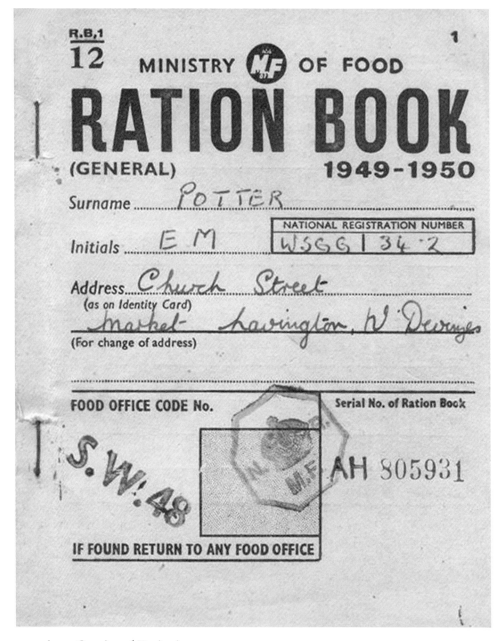

1949/50 – Continued Rationing

Rationing, so much a feature of total war, prevailed for the rest of the 1940s. Indeed, it was not until 1954 that meat and other food rationing came to an end. The reasons behind continued rationing were legion, including a number of adverse weather events that produced poor harvests – the harsh frosts of 1946/47 destroyed many potato stocks, forcing the vegetable onto the ration list. Industrial action at the ports throughout 1947 exacerbated the problem. Of course, the situation was not helped by the fact that Britain was now responsible for a large swathe of Europe that was unable to adequately feed itself.

1950S

'The Delicate Balance of Terror'

The 1950s in Britain was a period of relative stability. Rationing and national service – both hangovers from the Second World War – stopped in this period. Families aspired to owning a motor car and the economy was on the up. Harold Macmillan noted in a speech in Bradford in 1957,

> Indeed, let us be frank about it: most of our people have never had it so good. Go around the country, go to the industrial towns, go to the farms, and you will see a state of prosperity such as we have never had in my lifetime – nor indeed ever in the history of this country.
>
> Harold Macmillan, 20 July 1957

In reality, the economic recovery was due in part to the arms race that had been sparked by the realisation that Britain might well have to defend itself against aggression in the East. Nor did Britain want to lose its place at the United Nations Security Council, and the best way to preserve this was to continue the development of an independent nuclear deterrent. To do this, a whole new range of advanced delivery systems were needed: the V-force. By the end of the decade, the possibility of the United Kingdom being irreparably damaged by hydrogen bombs seemed almost inevitable.

8 October 1950 – Washingtons Plug the Bomber Gap, Exercise Emperor

A number of advanced, high altitude, nuclear-capable aircraft were being designed by the turn of the decade, though they were not to come into service for a further five years. Designs were also advanced in the production of Britain's first nuclear device, so much so that it looked like the RAF would have nothing capable of delivering the 'bomb'. From 1950, a number of refurbished B-29s were delivered to the RAF. Known as the Washington 88 aircraft, they eventually joined the service, replacing the ageing and increasingly dated Avro Lincoln.

1950 – The Korean War, Prelude to War in Europe? A T-34 Tank on a Bridge Destroyed by UN Forces Airstrike

On 25 June 1950, Communist-controlled North Korea, under Kim Il Sung, launched a surprise attack on its southern neighbour. The North Koreans were armed with Soviet T-34 tanks, Yak fighter aircraft and supported by Soviet military advisors. Two days later, the United Nations Security Council condemned the attack. The United States committed forces to the area the same day, with the United Kingdom following suit a month later. Many in the West saw the invasion as a prelude to war in Europe, and the conflict sparked a massive rearmament programme in Britain. ([*Army*] *NARA FILE: 111-C-6143 WAR & CONFLICT BOOK: 1499*)

Above: 1951 – War Room Construction Programme, Reading

In light of the uncertainties facing Britain, the British Government set about constructing a viable network of protected sites for Regional Commissioners. Intended to protect the Commissioner and staff during an attack, the team would then coordinate the efforts of the Civil Defence Corps in a rescue attempt. Sixteen such war rooms, as they quickly became known, had been built by 1954.

Opposite above: 1950 – British Troops in Action, Korea

Commandoes of the 41st Royal Marines plant demolition charges along railroad tracks of the enemy supply line, which they later demolished during a Commando raid, 8 miles south of Songjin, Korea. (*NARA FILE #: 80-G-428242*)

Opposite below: 1950 – British Commandos with their Korean Interpreter at 1st Marine Engineer Battalion Command Post, Korea

Britain committed nearly 15,000 troops to the United Nations force; 1,109 were never to return. Deaths on all sides were recently estimated to be in the region of 1.2 million. Those who continue to suggest the Cold War had few casualties would do well to remember this figure. (*Courtesy Sgt J.W. Helms Jnr, NARA FILE: 127-GK-234H-A5314*)

(NY8-Oct.23)FIRST OFFICIAL PICTURE OF BRITISH A-BOMB--This is the
first official picture of the detonation of the British atom bomb
at the Monte Bello Islands off the northwest Australian coast on
Oct.3rd. This is an early stage of the explosion after the initial
orange flash had been enveloped by the great uprush of water,clouds
of steam,smoke and spray.(APWirephoto)(b51055BIS)1952

Left: 3 October 1952 – Hurricane

Britain's first atomic device was detonated in Main Bay close to the Trimouille Island at 09:30 on 3 October. The device had been contained in the depths of a redundant River Class frigate – HMS *Plym*. Timescales were tight to say the least. Production of weapons-grade plutonium had taken far longer than expected. The reactors at Windscale, Cumbria, built specifically for the job, managed to fly out just enough material the day before the detonation. The event was seen as a national triumph, the culmination of five years' work – Britain had earned its place at the 'Top Table'.

Below left: 1952 – Royal Observer Corps 'B Type' Orlit Post Teignmouth, Devon

Two versions were built: a ground level structure and another which stood on 6-foot concrete legs for extra visibility. The construction programme was completed in 1955, the same year that missile and jet technology rendered the ROC obsolete.

Opposite page: 1952 – Royal Observer Corps 'A Type' Orlit Post, Fareham, Surrey

Until 1952, the Royal Observer Corps had reclaimed the old Second World War structures as observation posts; however, many were in a very poor state. In 1952, the Air Ministry approved the construction of over 400 'Orlit' posts – prefabricated structures in which plotting instrumentation could be used and stored.

1 November 1952 – Ivy Mike

Ivy Mike was the first fusion (hydrogen) device to be successfully detonated by the United States. The device, seen here, weighed in at 82 tons, partially due to a large refrigeration plant needed to keep liquid deuterium below 23.5 Kelvin. Within nine months, the Soviet Union had tested an air deliverable device. The Soviet test prompted Winston Churchill to describe the unfolding situation as a 'delicate balance of terror'. Britain's test of her first atomic weapon the month before now looked decidedly second rate.

1953 – Bedford RLHZ Self Propelled Pump – the Green Goddess

The Green Goddess is one of the most recognisable pieces of equipment from the whole of the Cold War. Over 5,000 were produced between 1953 and 1956. The Green Goddess was not strictly a fire engine, more a transportable pump capable of moving 900 gallons a minute at 100 psi. It was painted green so that it could be identified from local authority equipment that was the more usual red.

1953 – Blue Danube, Britain's First Air Deliverable Nuclear Weapon

By November 1953, the Royal Air Force gained nuclear capability when it took delivery of Blue Danube. The weapon was large and difficult to handle; at over 7.5 m long and weighing over 4,500 kg, the RAF's largest bomber, the Valiant, only just managed to carry the payload. Nevertheless, this low yield (10–12 Kt) fission weapon still provided Britain with a truly independent deterrent.

Above: 1953 – Stalin Dies

On 5 March, Joseph Stalin finally succumbed to a stroke he had suffered three days earlier. Such was his reign of fear, it took nearly a day to find a doctor who would initially tend to him. It seemed the world could breathe a little easier on his passing.

Right: Khrushchev Ascends

Stalin's successor, Nikita Sergeyevich Khrushchev, seen here with Fidel Castro, while not having Stalin's appetite for executions, would still manage to push the world to the brink of nuclear warfare. He would also oversee a series of disastrous agricultural policies, several of which the Soviet Union never recovered from.

Above: 1955 – Vickers-Armstrong Valiant Enters Service

The first of the now famous V-Force aircraft, the Vickers-Armstrong Valiant, entered service with the Royal Air Force on 8 February 1955 – first with No. 232 Operational Conversion Unit at RAF Gaydon, and shortly afterwards with No. 138 Squadron. Just over 100 aircraft were to see service with the RAF. The aircraft performed the first trials for the burgeoning nuclear deterrent. Coupled with the Blue Danube, it was Britain's first true independent weapons system.

Opposite above and below: 1955 – The Strath Report

Nuclear tests by both the USA and Soviet Union were demonstrating the development of more powerful weapons, some of which were being targeted on the United Kingdom. Currently, Britain had developed a defensive capability around the atomic bomb with its limited (if still awesome) power. Towards the end of 1954, the government set up a committee of civil servants in secret. They were to assess the likelihood of Britain surviving an attack using the H-bomb. The report was published in 1955, with Strath concluding the danger to Britain from the effects of radioactive fallout alone would be all but unmanageable. The report immediately rendered the entire British civil defence effort impotent.

    The Strath report sounded the death knell for the Civil Defence Corps. Rescue from any area struck by a hydrogen weapon would be almost impossible. Volunteers continued to train, but over the next decade the organisation would find it difficult to remain relevant in a rapidly changing world.

14 May 1955 – Warsaw Pact Formed

On 9 May 1955, West Germany is admitted to NATO. Initially, the French objected to admittance; however, the threat from the East was far greater and eventually they relented to membership. Naturally, the Soviets classed this as evidence of NATO aggression and formalised the Treaty of Friendship, Cooperation, and Mutual Assistance, a collective defence treaty in Central and Eastern Europe. On 14 May, the Warsaw Pact was born. While the Pact was outwardly intended to counter the 'threat' from NATO, it also meant Moscow could consolidate control of satellite countries by having large air and ground forces stationed on their territory.

1956 – The Hungarian Uprising

In the most serious challenge yet to direct Soviet rule, students in the Hungarian capital, Budapest, marched in defiance of the local communist party on 23 October. The following day, Soviet armoured units entered the city and hundreds dies over the next few days, a general ceasefire coming into force by 30 October. Imre Nagy was placed in charge of an interim government; by 1 November he had abandoned the one-party system, requested withdrawal from the Warsaw Pact and asked the UN to recognise Hungary as a truly independent state. This was too much for Khrushchev, who mobilised 4,000 tanks massed on the border. Fierce street fighting cost the lives of nearly 3,000, and it took two weeks to finally crush the uprising.

1956 – Egyptian Prisoners, Suez 'Operation Musketeer'

In 1956, the Egyptian Government nationalised the Suez Canal, and in so doing threatened substantial financial and strategic investments owned by France and Britain. A joint operation was devised in which Israeli forces would invade Sinai while the Anglo-French taskforce would seize the canal. Public and international opinion were misjudged, the action was severely condemned by the United Nations, and the United States forced Britain, through economic and financial sanctions, to withdraw just six weeks into the operation.

1957 – Avro Vulcan Enters Service

Arguably the most iconic British aircraft of the Cold War, the Avro Vulcan officially entered service with the Royal Air Force on 21 February (although deliveries had been made from September 1956). The 'tin triangle', as it became known in aviation circles, was in RAF service until March 1984. The Mk 2 version of this aircraft had a top speed of 0.98 mach at 55,000 feet and an operational ceiling of over 60,000 feet. The Vulcan performed a number of roles throughout its operational life, but by far the most deadly was the role it played in Britain's nuclear deterrent.

1957 – The Corporal Battlefield Nuclear Weapon Enters Service

Operated by the Royal Artillery 47th Guided Weapons Regiment in West Germany from 1957, the missile had an estimated range of around 130 km, but was extremely unreliable, the British test fire success being less than 50 per cent. This was the first tactical nuclear weapon deployed by the British Army.

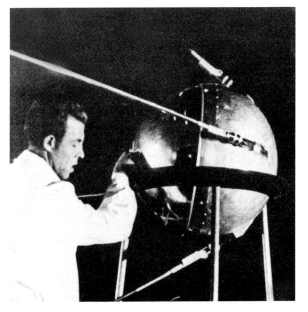

1957 – Sputnik

On 4 October 1957, the Soviet Union was publicly credited with placing the first man-made object in space. This was a huge blow to the Americans, as not only had they been relegated into second place in what became the 'Space Race', but this also meant the Soviet Union had a credible ballistic missile programme capable of threatening all NATO members – including Britain.

1957 – Grapple X, Britain's First Hydrogen Weapon Test

Britain conducted a number of atmospheric tests in 1957/58 at Christmas Island in the Pacific Ocean. On 8 November 1957, a Vickers Valiant piloted by Sqn Ldr B. Millet dropped the UK's first true thermonuclear device, achieving a yield of 1.8 megatons. By April 1958, a 3-megaton yield had been achieved. Now the United States began negotiations for a resumption of technical co-operation. Veterans, who once viewed involvement with a sense of national pride, continue to suffer from the effects of these trials.

1957 – Handley Page Victor Enters Service

At the end of November, the last of the V-force types, the Victor, entered service with the Royal Air Force. The aircraft was capable of carrying a massive payload, up to 48,000 lbs – twice that of the Vulcan – over 3,300 miles. Now the V-force was complete. What the fleet really needed was a weapon that complemented this awesome capability, but it would have to wait until 1962 for that.

February 1958 – Campaign for Nuclear Disarmament

By 1958, it was clear that the world was becoming an increasingly dangerous place. At a meeting in the Conway Hall in London a new, public-faced organisation was formed – Campaign for Nuclear Disarmament (CND) – intended to enact civil disobedience rather than outward violent opposition. Peace rallies ensued, including an annual Easter March from Trafalgar Square to Aldermaston. Tony Benn later remarked, 'They were a nice, keen crowd, though mainly middle-class – one of CND's greatest weaknesses.' The widely recognised peace symbol was designed for CND that year by Gerald Holtom. The symbol prevails to this day.

Opposite above: 1958 – Government Advice – Too Little Too Late

Throughout the late 1950s, the government began producing literature that was intended to provide the necessary information to ensure survival. The newly formed CND had a field day.

Opposite below: 1958 – Royal Observer Corps Moves Underground

The Strath report called for a country-wide organisation to be set up with the intent of monitoring radioactive fallout should an attack come. The ideal candidates were the Royal Observer Corps. Their aircraft observation role had been reduced in effectiveness ever since jet aircraft had been introduced, and with the steady growth in missile technology it looked like the ROC's days were numbered. They were drafted into a new organisation, United Kingdom Warning and Monitoring Organisation (UKWMO), as the organisation's field force. To protect against radiation, each team was provided with an Underground Monitoring Post. (*Courtesy Malcolm Holland*)

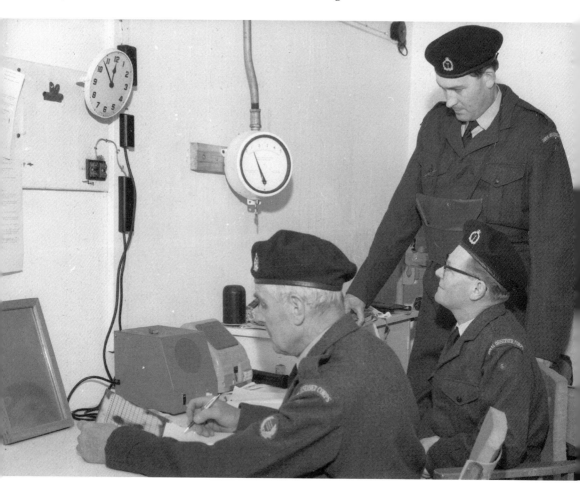

1958 – Royal Observer Corps Moves Underground

Each post had space for three observers to operate for up to two weeks, isolated from the world outside. Their task was to record the direction, bomb power and radiation footprint from a nuclear detonation. This was then passed to a Group Headquarter, who informed the military and Home Office of the facts of the event. (*Courtesy Malcolm Holland*)

Opposite above: 1958 – Royal Observer Corps Moves Underground

Opening the Group 5 HQ Bunker at Watford. From here warnings would be given to the military and other authorities about the imminent arrival of radioactive fallout.

Opposite below: 1958 – Thunderbird Missile Deployed with Royal Artillery

The Thunderbird missile was delivered to the Royal Artillery after extensive trials at RAE Aberporth, West Wales and Woomera, Australia. The ground-to-air missile combined mobility with potency, able to bring down a target over 40 km away. The weapons system saw service until 1977.

1958 – 'Project Emily', the Arrival of Thor

From the mid-1950s, the United States became entwined in a ballistic missile arms race. The aim was to develop an Intercontinental Ballistic Missile (ICBM) capable of striking the Soviet Union from home territory. The weapons systems would take time to develop and a large missile gap was appearing due to the Soviet Union stationing missiles capable of threatening European and Japanese targets. Intermediate Range Ballistic Missiles (IRBM) were the answer; the problem was they needed to be stationed close to their targets (relatively speaking). In February 1958, it was agreed that the RAF would take delivery of the Thor missile system, and the first flights were installed at RAF Feltwell in September 1958. With their arrival, Britain secured itself as a main Soviet target.

Opposite page: 1958 – Bloodhound Enters Service with RAF

The Bloodhound missile was one of the Cold War's most enduring weapons systems, enjoying over thirty years of service both in the United Kingdom and with foreign forces. The Bloodhound's introduction was one requirement of Project Emily, intended to guard the launch bases along the east coast of England. The ground-to-air missile had a down range capability of 185 km and ceiling of 20,000+. (*Department of Defence Imagery photo no. DF-ST-83-00493*)

1959 – The Beginning of the End

By the end of the decade it was clear that an attack on the United Kingdom would most probably comprise nuclear weapons – especially the H-bomb. A new generation was also rejecting the concept of civil defence in the face of the threat. There was a subsequent downturn in recruitment into the Civil Defence Corps (CDC), and eventually the British Government would disband the majority of services.

1960s

The Nuclear Clock Approaches Midnight

If the 1950s had been a period where new, ever more powerful weapons had been developed, the 1960s was the decade when they came closest to being deployed. World tensions over Cuba in 1962 brought the planet to the brink of disaster. For a while, the British independent deterrent was on full standby – the only time the Royal Observer Corps was placed on alert in its Cold War history. Between 22–28 October 1962, both the United States and Soviet Union had their fingers firmly on the trigger. After the crisis had died down, a 'hotline' was installed between Washington and Moscow. The events led a leading academic and founder of CND to note:

> Anyone who requires new material for nightmares should bear in mind the following statements which have been made by men in positions of critical responsibility.
> Admiral Radford: 'I demand … total victory over the Communist system – not stalemate.'
> General Nathan Twining: 'If it were not for the politicians I would settle the war in one afternoon by bombing Soviet Russia.'
> The sombre conclusion is that, unless the politics of the Great Powers are radically changed within the next few years, the chances of human survival are very slight.
> Bertrand Russell, *The Accidental War*, 1962

The event also highlighted just how vulnerable the public in Britain were. CND membership increased rapidly and a number of regional government headquarters were vandalised. The 1960s were a turning point. No longer would there be blind acceptance of nuclear warfare.

1960 – English Electric Lightning Enters Service

Throughout the preceding decade, the Soviet Union had been developing a fleet of high-level long-range bombers, capable of reaching the United Kingdom. The RAF's missile systems were now equipped with Bloodhound, although it was preferable to destroy aircraft miles from your border rather than over your country. The Lightning fulfilled that role. The aircraft entered frontline service on 11 July 1960, providing the RAF with a supersonic interceptor capable of a 65,000-foot ceiling.

Opposite page: 1960 – Gary Powers

On the 1 May 1960, a U-2 spy plane, piloted by Francis Gary Powers, was shot down by a surface-to-air missile while deep in Soviet territory. Powers survived and was sentenced to ten years in prison, although he was exchanged in Berlin twenty-one months later. Afterwards, political relations sank to an all-time low. In Britain, the Royal Air Force had to completely revise its tactics; the V-force could no longer rely on height to keep them out of harm's way as Powers' U-2 had been at an altitude of 23,000+ metres when hit. As no apology was forthcoming from the West, Khrushchev walked out of ongoing nuclear test ban talks in Paris.

12 April 1961 – First Man in Space

As if the humiliation of Sputnik had not been enough, on 12 April Major Yuri Gagarin became the first man in space. He became internationally famous overnight with events thrown in his honour around the world – further rubbing America's nose in it. His success was to be short-lived; Gagarin never returned to space and was unfortunately killed in a training exercise on 27 March 1968.

1961 – Yellow Sun Mk II

When the RAF took delivery of the aptly named Yellow Sun Mk II, Britain finally had a true strategic thermonuclear weapon capability. The casing was large, at 6.4 m in length, although this was deceptive – the physics package was a fraction of the size. The weapon had a yield of 1.1 megatons. It was to be delivered via the V-force. (*RAF Hendon*)

17 April 1961 – Bay of Pigs

In January 1959, the '26 July Movement', led by Fidel Castro, finally forced the collapse of Dictator General Batista's regime in Cuba. He immediately set about confiscating American-owned businesses and removing the American Government's influence from the island nation. The new regime was not intentionally communist, and was initially more socialist in outlook. This changed when Batista exiles, supported by the CIA, attempted to invade the island on 17 April 1961. The 'Bay of Pigs' incident was a disaster for the USA and drove Cuba closer to Moscow. By late 1962, the alliance would drive the world to the brink of nuclear war. (*Library of Congress Prints and Photographs Division Washington, DC 20540*)

Left: 13 August 1961 – Berlin Wall

For over fifteen years, people, many of them
skilled, had fled across the porous border that
divided the city of Berlin. By the late 1950s, it
was clear that western powers were not intending
to leave the city, so the East German authorities
moved to stem the flow out of the country.
The Anti-Fascist Protection Rampart, as it was
promoted in the East, was the brainchild of Erich
Honecker, later leader of the DDR.

Below: 1961 – Berlin, the Divided City

The Berlin Wall became the symbol of a divided
Europe, the epitome of Churchill's 'Iron Curtain'
made physical. It also demonstrated that the
Soviet-backed authority was not about to take the
rest of Berlin by force.

27/28 October 1961 – The First and Only Time Soviet and American Tanks Faced Each Other Down, Checkpoint Charlie, Berlin

Even though a wall had just been constructed, the four occupying forces in Berlin had unrestricted access into each other's administrative areas. That was until US Chief of Mission in West Berlin, E. Allan Lightner, was stopped in his car at Checkpoint Charlie. By the evening of 27 October, both superpowers had deployed tanks in the city, with ten from each side 'facing off' at the border control point. By eleven o'clock the following day, both NATO and Strategic Air Command were on full alert. This was the only time Soviet and American tanks faced each other in the entire Cold War.

1961 – 'Burlington', The Central Government Protected HQ at Corsham

In development for over five years, the Second World War aero engine factory and adjacent quarries at Corsham in Wiltshire were, by late 1961, able to accept up to 7,000 civil servants employed on war duties. They would not deal with the general public but were built to authorise nuclear retaliation should the need arise. Entrance to the site was via lifts and escalators; this one had been taken from Holborn underground station in London. (© *Crown Copyright, Press Release series by MOD DLO/DPA photography and video dept., Foxhill, Bath*)

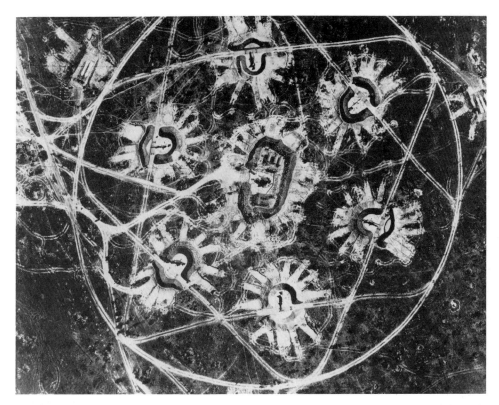

1962 – The Cuban Missile Crisis, U-2 image of a SAM-4 Site in Cuba

After the Bay of Pigs incident, the US Government imposed swingeing sanctions on the Castro Government, including the refusal to accept sugar cane from the island. Moscow was only too happy to oblige, and Khrushchev also saw an opportunity to station nuclear weapons literally in the 'yard of the United States'. This was not provocative; the US had stationed Jupiter missiles in Turkey and Italy already. Construction of several launch pads started in late summer; by 14 October, a U-2 aircraft had confirmed the existence of the work. The US Government undertook a naval blockade and when a U-2 was shot down and several ships carrying nuclear weapons tried to run the blockade, it looked like war was imminent. Thankfully, an agreement was brokered at the United Nations – both sides dismantling their weapons. (*US Department of Defence*)

Opposite above: 'Burlington' Air Vent

To ensure the underground populus was provided with safe breathing air, a massive air filtration system was developed, capable of removing radioactive particles and chemicals from the atmosphere. (© *Crown Copyright, Press Release series by MOD DLO/DPA photography and video dept., Foxhill, Bath*)

Opposite below: 'Burlington' Communications Network

NATO financed the retention and servicing of a 'clockwork' telephone network around the United Kingdom. It was less susceptible to the electromagnetic pulse pumped out from a nuclear detonation. (© *Crown Copyright, Press Release series by MOD DLO/DPA photography and video dept., Foxhill, Bath*)

1962 – Oxford City Control

At the beginning of the decade, the government had indicated that a number of Civil Defence regions would be provided with up-to-date controls. This large, two-storey blockhouse was built on the edge of Oxford on Woodstock Road and demonstrates something of the utilitarian appearance of certain structures.

Opposite above: 1963 – Blue Steel Enters Service

Design of a weapon able to increase the projection of the V-force's bombing power had started back in 1954. By 1962, the tested stand-off missile was being issued to the Royal Air Force and in February 1963, became operational. The weapon increased the potency of the V-force tenfold, forcing the Warsaw Pack member states to rethink their European strategy; a pre-emptive strike on British bases was now on the cards.

Opposite below: The Deadly Package

A Vulcan carrying the Blue Steel. This was the apogee of the British independent deterrent as operated by the Royal Air Force, and remained so for the rest of the decade. (*Courtesy Adrian Balch collection*)

17 September 1963 – Fylingdales becomes Operational

The Ballistic Missile Early Warning System at RAF Fylingdales, North Yorkshire – locally known as the 'Golf Balls' – were without doubt the most recognisable symbols of the nuclear threat to Britain. Taking three years to build, the station was commissioned on 17 September 1963. The United Kingdom Warning and Monitoring Organisation (UKWMO) was among the many recipients of information generated here. (*Scarborough Evening News*)

The Golf Balls: A Tourist Attraction

Bizarrely, the most important base in the United Kingdom quickly became a tourist attraction. The impressive domed structures set the backdrop for many postcards and family snaps throughout the 1960s and 1970s.

1963 – Fylingdales Radar

Underneath each 'Golf Ball' was a single, 25 m, parabolic scanner, 10 m high and weighing a massive 112 tonnes. The AN/FPS-49 radar was capable of spotting an object 4,500 km distant, so the moment one appeared above the horizon it was tracked. This would start the on-site calculation sequence and the clock running. (*Scarborough Evening News*)

1963 – Fylingdales Threat Report

As an object appeared over the horizon it was tracked by the massive radar arrays – speed, height and inclination were all fed into an impact predictor. This then calculated the impact area using a number of preset scenarios, including type of weapon and apogee; this was then fed to the Threat Report Board in the Fylingdales operations room, whereupon the senior officer would pass the information to the Home Office. Note the Threat Report Board is covered in this press picture. The countdown it provided is the origin of the 'Four Minute Warning'. (*Scarborough Evening News*)

1963 – WE-177 Series Enters Service

Intended to be the primary weapon for the cancelled TSR2, the WE-177 is Britain's longest-serving nuclear weapon. Three versions were in service between 1963 and 1998, with both the Royal Navy as a depth charge and the RAF as a free-fall bomb in both kiloton and megaton ranges. The performance of the WE-177 is still classified, but what is known is that even though the weapon is only a tenth of the size of Blue Danube, it had a thousand times the destructive power. A multitude of aircraft could carry the weapon – it was ready for use in the European theatre by 1965.

1963–1967 – Aden Emergency, 37 Squadron Avro Shackleton Bombers

On 10 December 1964, a grenade was thrown at a group of British officials at Aden Airport, subsequently a state of emergency was declared in the Aden Protectorate. The Royal Air Force undertook a number of missions in the country, specifically the rebel stronghold of Radfan. The Avro Shckleton was used to conduct bombing runs across the area. *(Picture courtesy John A. Dorward Collection)*

15 October 1964 – Leonid Brezhnev, First Secretary

Initially sharing power with Alexei Kosygin (Prime Minister), Leonid Brezhnev's power base relied on a strong economy. Unfortunately, increases in military expenditure and prestige projects such as the space programme ensured living standards across the Soviet Union were well below those enjoyed in the West. This ensured that an underlying current of dissent permeated most of Soviet society, eventually leading to its downfall.

1966 – The Chieftain Battle Tank

In 1966, the first forty chieftain battle tanks were issued to the British Army. This potent field weapon fired 120 mm shells and was fully Nuclear, Chemical, Biological (NBC) protected. It was stationed widely throughout Germany with the British Army of the Rhine (BAOR) until the end of the Cold War. It also sold well to a number of Middle Eastern countries.

1967 – Six-Day War: Israeli Armour Heads Towards the Sinai to Counter Egyptian Formations Massing There

Between 5–10 June, Israeli forces took on the numerically superior Egyptian military machine. The Egyptians had been massing troops on the border, and there had been a period of tension with both Syria and Jordan. Within six days, the Israelis won decisive victories over all three. More importantly, the Israeli Air Force had destroyed much of the Egyptian Air Force on the ground – suddenly parking aircraft outside in rows was not such a good idea. NATO took note and subsequently changed the British landscape by hardening up a number of airfields.

1963–1967 – Members of the Federal Regular Army at Dhala, Aden.

Initially a police operation, by late 1967, the British had lost control and were under sporadic attack from a number of independent groups. With anti-British feeling spreading throughout the region, the withdrew. Throughout 1967, the RAF evacuated over 6,000 civilians and, in the last week of the operation, 3,700 military and a further 350 civilians were evacuated by air. *(Picture courtesy John A. Dorward Collection)*

15 June 1968 – First Polaris Patrol

Britain's nuclear capability, until the launch of the first Polaris submarine HMS *Resolution*, had had one major flaw – it had neither the element of surprise nor that of stealth. A first strike would almost certainly wipe out the deterrent. On 15 June 1968, the first Polaris patrol changed all that and, from 1969, the responsibility for delivering British nuclear weapons, should they be needed, passed to the Royal Navy.

April 1968 – The Abandonment of Civil Defence

After twenty years of preparing for warfare, initially against mounting odds from more powerful weapons, but increasingly through anti-nuclear public opinion, Whitehall decided to pull the funding for the Civil Defence Corps, Auxiliary Fire Service and a range of other voluntary forces. The problem was the organisation never really shed the misnomer that strong cups of tea would save the day, especially with the horror of the H-bomb. The public were now very much 'on their own' if warfare came.

Above: **Polaris Patrol.**

A rare shot of a missile tube open.

Left: **Polaris Launch.**

A test firing of a Polaris missile in 1982 off the coast of Florida from a submerged HMS *Revenge. (Department of Defence Image DF-SC-84-04513)*

Spring 1968 – Prague

At the beginning of 1968, the Czechoslovakian administration began a series of reforms specifically aimed at decentralising a failing internal economy. Leonid Brezhnev met with the Czech leader, Alexander Dubcek, on 3 August, demanding he stop the reforms immediately. Seventeen days later, Warsaw Pact troops poured over the border, crushing the hopes of millions. The West protested but had no way of intervening. (© *Vladimir Lammer, Wenceslas Square, Prague, 1968*)

1968 – Devizes Civil Defence Control

Not all protected structures were what they appeared to be at first glance. Sheep Street in Devizes was redeveloped in the 1960s. During this work, the town was treated to a new library. The above ground structure was indeed a library, but built in such a way that, should it collapse, it would not damage the large bunker underneath.

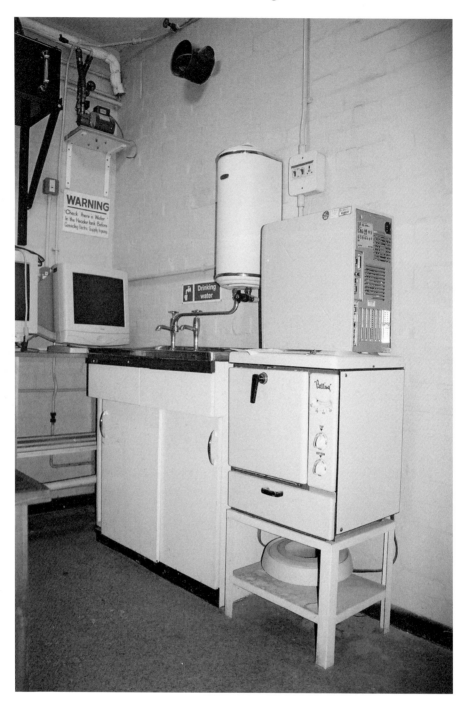

/CBEL1641454-8/15/69-BELFAST, N. IRELAND: In a scene reminiscent of World War II, British ops take over Falls Road area here 8/15 following a day of savage violence in which three sons were reported killed by gun fire during rioting. UPI CABLEPHOTO =hgr BEL*502

15 August 1969 – First Troop Deployment in Northern Ireland, Troops on the Falls Road

After years of institutionalised discrimination against the Catholic minority, tensions finally reached breaking point. By 1968, this had reached crisis point and, on 5 October, a clash between an Orange Order march and the Northern Ireland Civil Rights association became the first such televised across the United Kingdom. Violence spread the following year and on 14 August 1969, the first British troops were deployed to separate the Nationalists and Loyalists, the following day they were embroiled in the dispute. (*UPI Cablephoto = hgr BEL*502*)

Opposite page: 1968 – Devizes Civil Defence Control

A small kitchen served to provide meals for the thirty or so staff that would have run the bunker during an emergency. The structure was opened the same year the Civil Defence Corps was disbanded; however, the facility was important enough to continue. The bunker remained in use until the early 1990s, and the library is still in use today.

(NY38-Aug.20)CLEANUP---British troops operate bulldozer to clear debris and barricades away Wednesday in Belfast, Northern Ireland, as calm returned to the city after the recent rioting there.(See AP Wire Story by Colin Frost)(APWIREPHOTO)via Cable from Belfast) (jb41620pw)1969

20 August 1969 – First Troop Deployment in Northern Ireland. British Troops Cleaning Up After a Night of Rioting

Initially sympathetic to the plight of the Catholics, the troops soon learnt that they were to become the focus of much of the hatred vented on the loyalists. Rather than be seen as a peacekeeping force, they were considered an occupying force. (*Colin Frost APWIREPHOTO jb41620pw 1969*)

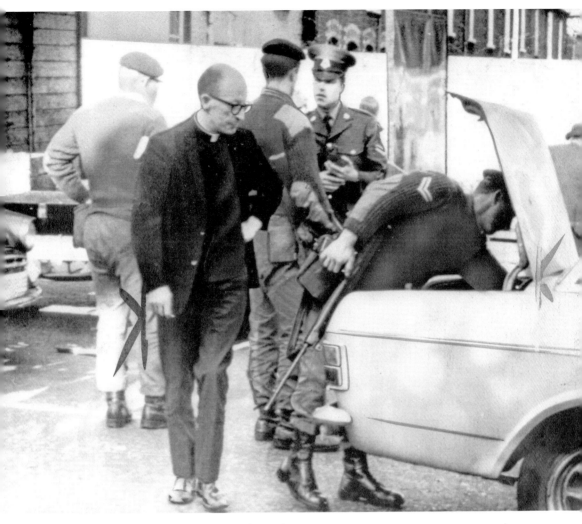

Military Inspections: No One Was Above the Law

Entry to the Falls Road area was restricted by the British troops. Anyone moving in or out (especially if driving) was searched. By September, it appeared that the only way to reduce the violence was to segregate both sides. The caption for this photograph, taken on 9 September, says it all: 'Troops are working to complete the "Belfast Wall" a steel and barbed wire fence designed to separate the Roman Catholic and Protestant areas.' (*AP Wirephoto by cable from Belfast hrm70842pw*)

1970s

The Troublesome Decade

The 1970s have always been considered the decade of détente, the decade where quarrels were put aside and friendships created. From the outside, this would be correct. The Space Race settled into a number of joint operations and the decade was punctuated by arms deals and talk of the reduction of nuclear forces across the world.

Nothing could have been further from the truth. This was the period when the most deadly chemical weapons were developed, the neutron bomb was devised and possibly deployed in Europe, and both sides sought to use the recently signed deals to deploy more accurate nuclear systems. By the end of the decade, a war would break out that has been on the boil ever since.

1971 – First British Soldier Killed in the Troubles, 6 February. A Woman is Taken into Custody After Riots in Newry, 25 October

After more than eighteen months of intervening between warring factions in Northern Ireland, it was inevitable that a British soldier would be killed. That same year, internment was reintroduced and the number of troops on the street steadily increased. By 1972, 28,000 troops were deployed across the region. After the soldier's death and during an increase in violence, anyone suspected was dragged in for questioning. (*APWIREPHOTO pr20922pw 1971*)

1972 – Strategic Arms Limitation Talks (SALT 1)

The Strategic Arms Limitation Talks Agreement (SALT 1) froze the number of strategic ballistic missile launchers at existing levels and allowed new systems to be introduced at the expense of removing older systems from theatre. The accord was signed by Richard Nixon and Leonid Brezhnev on 26 May at a summit in Moscow. By mid-1974, Nixon's Presidency was in tatters, and he resigned on 9 August. (*Culver Pictures Inc.*)

14 October 1973 – Yom Kippur War, Soldiers Taking Cover in Their Foxholes in the Sands of Southern Sinai

In an attempt to win back territory ceded in 1967 to Israel, both Syrian and Egyptian forces launched attacks into occupied territory. By 25 October, a UN force was patrolling the disputed areas and the Egyptian and Israeli governments were in direct talks. Moreover, the subsequent support for Israel by the United States was a direct cause of the Organisation of the Petroleum Exporting Countries (OPEC) reduction in production, damaging many estern countries through the energy crisis. (*Israeli Government Press Office, Image No. D334-122*)

21 November 1973 – Yom Kippur War, Prime Minister Golda Meir and Defence Minister Moshe Dayan and Aluf Hoffi Speaking to Troops on the Golan Heights

The war also set back superpower relations as both sides were now starting to supply governments of favour with weaponry. In an attempt to exert influence, the Soviet Union supplied the Egyptian and Syrian governments – a legacy still with us today – while the United States finally cemented its support for an Israeli nation. (*Israeli Government Press Office, Photographer Frenkel Ron Image No. D334-092*)

23 November 1974 – Gerald Ford Arrives in Vladivostok

Conscious that the SALT 1 treaty would run out in 1977, both East and West were looking for a more encompassing accord – one that would truly reduce the amount of nuclear weapons both sides currently maintained. Shortly after taking office, President Ford organised a meeting to discuss the structure of such an agreement. The Vladivostok Summit Meeting on Arms Control took place over 23/24 November. Both sides agreed to maintain parity in their stockpiles. (*White House Photograph Courtesy Gerald R. Ford Library-A2102-06-600*)

Top: 14 August 1974 – First Flight of Tornado

The Panavia Tornado was a multi-role combat aircraft designed by the European consortium Panavia. Bringing together aeronautical expertise from Germany, Italy and Britain, the variable geometry aircraft had an outstanding low flying capacity and nuclear capability. By the mid-1980s, over 700 were in operation across Europe. Nearly 1,000 were built in all. (*National Archive# NN33300514 2005-06-30*)

Middle: 1975 – Lance for the British Army on the Rhine

The 50th Missile Regiment Royal Artillery was re-equipped with the Lance Missile System in mid-1975. Lance was capable of carrying conventional, chemical or nuclear warheads and remained the principle tactical weapon in Germany until their withdrawal as part of the INF Treaties a decade later. (*Department of Defense Imagery photo no. DA-SC-88-01650*)

Below: 1975 – Belize Harrier Deployment

Belize, formally British Honduras, was granted self-governance in 1964, although the English-speaking country wished to retain the Queen as Head of State. British Honduras was officially renamed Belize in 1973. Unfortunately, territorial demands were placed on the country by neighbouring Guatemala. A Harrier Squadron and around 1,500 troops were detached to Belize in 1975, and were stationed there for the remainder of the Cold War. (*Courtesy Pete Butt*)

1975 – Fall of Saigon

By the beginning of 1975, it was clear the combined efforts of the United States armed services were no match for a well supplied, ingenious and fanatical guerrilla army. For the communist governments around the world, this was more than a victory of arms – it had demonstrated to the world that communism could, and would, prevail – often in the face of seemingly insurmountable odds.

17 July 1975 – Soyuz-Apollo Test Project

On 17 July, a United States Apollo module docked, via a specialised module, with a Soviet Soyuz module. Promoted as a mission to test out the docking system and pave the way for more joint endeavours, the world saw it as a symbol of détente – peace was definitely in the air. Little did the public know that in the background both sides were developing even more deadly chemical and nuclear weapons – détente was no more than a political umbrella to cover weapons development. (*NASA S75-22410 March 1975*)

1976 – Deployment of the SS-20 Intermediate Range Ballistic Missile (IMRBM)

As if to underpin the true nature of détente, the Soviet Government increased the stakes by deploying a mobile nuclear platform, the SS-20, across central Europe. Its lethality lay in the system's all-terrain mobility, making it virtually impossible to find once deployed in the field (remember how difficult it was to locate SCUD launchers in Iraq fifteen years later?). The Cold War began to heat up from this point. (*DoD D-ST-85-06624 Artists Impression*)

This booklet tells you how to make your home and your family as safe as possible under nuclear attack

1976 – *Protect and Survive* is Published

The civil defence publication *Protect and Survive*, synonymous with Margaret Thatcher, was actually published three years before she came to office by Jim Callaghan's Labour government. After the disbandment of the Civil Defence Corps in 1968, the public had been left pretty much on their own, but now here was a booklet full of help, should the worst happen – CND and others had a field day!

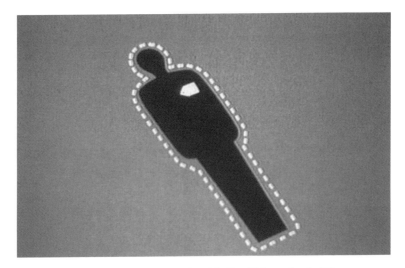

1976 – *Protect and Survive*: What To Do if Somebody Dies

To accompany the release of the *Protect and Survive* booklet, a number of public information films were also released. Ironically narrated by Patrick Allen, the voice of Barratt Homes at the time, they expanded on how to protect yourself and your family. Allen would later find fame when he collaborated with *Frankie Goes To Hollywood's* epic *Two Tribes* track.

16 October 1978 – Pope John Paul II

Born Karol Józef Wojtyła, Pope John Paul II was inaugurated on 22 October. Of Polish descent, he was the first non-Italian pope for 455 years. A major supporter of human rights, he supported the efforts of Lech Wałesa, the founder and leader of Solidarity, eventually bringing about a governmental change in Poland, and was widely recognised as the catalyst for the dismantling of communist regimes across Europe.

Left: 1979 – Agreement to Station Pershing and GLCMs in Europe

In an attempt to counter the threat posed by the deployment of the SS-20s, NATO requested an upgrade to existing tactical nuclear weapons stationed in Europe. By 1979, they had that commitment from the United States. The Pershing II missiles were to be deployed from mobile launchers similar to the SS-20. (*Pershing II missiles in Germany – Andrew Law*)

Below: 3 May 1979 – The Conservative Victory

When the Conservatives swept to power in May 1979, nobody could have predicted the effect the first female British Prime Minister would have on the world stage. Margaret Thatcher was formidable, earning the name the 'Iron Lady' from the Soviet Premie,r and facing down the IRA and what she considered the wastefulness of Europe.

DOMESTIC NUCLEAR SHELTERS

Advice on
domestic shelters
providing protection
against
nuclear explosions

A Home Office guide

December 1979 – Home Defence Review

With tensions building in Europe over the stationing of new medium-range ballistic missiles across the Continent by both sides, the newly returned Thatcher government set about implementing a new Home Defence policy. When the report was delivered in early 1980, it recommended a three-fold increase in funding, intended to produce a more effective level of civil preparedness. It also recommended a complete refurbishment of the bunker system around the United Kingdom.

December 1979 – Invasion of Afghanistan

On or around Christmas Day 1979, huge numbers of Soviet infantry and tanks moved over the border into Afghanistan. President Carter, in the State of the Union address a few weeks later, talked of nuclear weapons being an option – thankfully that was not to be. The resilience of local fighters, such as those pictured here (Sayyaf group Mujahideen in Jaji, Paktia, Afghanistan, August 1984), ensured that the Red Army encountered resistance specially equipped and trained by the CIA.

1980s

'When Two Tribes Go to War One is All that You Can Score'

The 1980s ushered in a far more deadly period through the stationing of superpower weapons in Europe. To the majority of the population, it appeared that both sides had agreed to hold a limited war in Central Europe rather than face annihilation of their own countries. Civil disobedience rose to new heights, the peace camps around cruise bases became centres for violent political dissent, and further groups began camping out at most military sites across the United Kingdom. Parodying the recently released *Alien* film, CND noted: 'From America No One Can Hear You Scream.'

However, this was also a decade of change, in the Soviet Union at least. The old guard was replaced by a new man with a new message. The people of his country would benefit from consumer goods, hospitals would be rebuilt, education brought up to scratch and nuclear weapons would be reduced. By the middle of the decade, it looked like the world was on a new track. Unfortunately, as the decade played out, many of the client groups armed by East and West in an attempt to court favour turned their weapons on their former masters.

1980 – Operation Eagle Claw, Tehran Rescue

On 24 April 1980, a military unit, later to become Delta Force, was ordered into Iran to rescue fifty-two American diplomats who had been held captive since November 1979. The operation was a disaster, eight men were killed, six helicopters and a C-130 Hercules were lost. It would be another nine months before the hostages were released. The event also damaged Jimmy Carter's presidency, paving the way for arguably the most influential president of the Cold War – Ronald Reagan.

17 June 1980 – Britain Announces Cruise Missile Bases

NATO's decision to modernise its intermediate range missile profile in Europe took a major step forward when, on 17 June, the then Secretary of State for Defence, Francis Pym, announced in the House of Commons that 160 cruise missiles would be based at two Royal Air Force stations. One, RAF Greenham Common, was to dominate the British anti-nuclear debate for the next decade. Six hardened shelters were constructed, each capable of housing two launch controls and four launch vehicles, equalling sixteen cruise missiles.

1980 – The Modernisation of the Home Defence Regions

While some plans had been drawn up in the mid-1970s, it took the Conservative government to get things moving. A modernisation of all levels of protected structures was initiated. One such work was the complete refurbishment of a radar operations room in Cheshire. Hack Green became a regional government headquarters, costing over £20 million.

Opposite above: 1980 – Strikes in Poland, the Rise of Solidarity

Throughout the 1970s, the Polish economy, like that of many other eastern bloc countries, was in crisis. A continual round of food price increases eventually led to mass strikes. From 14 August 1980, the country was at a standstill and the strikers, sensing something important was happening, formed Solidarity (Solidarnosc), which gained 10 million members within a year.

Opposite below: 1980 – Strikes in Poland

Solidarity leader, Lech Wałesa, was eventually imprisoned along with thousands of others as the government declared martial law. By 1989, the government was forced to negotiate and held semi-free elections. Pope John Paul II outwardly supported the movement, promoting the value of freedom in his native Poland and of those across Central Europe. This was the point at which the 'Iron Curtain' began to be breached.

5 November 1980 – The Rise of the Nuclear Free City

The steady rise in tension after the invasion of Afghanistan and clear rearming by both sides prompted many local and regional authorities to speak out. The first Nuclear Free Zone in the United Kingdom was declared by Manchester City Council on 5 November.

20 January 1981 – Ronald Reagan Becomes President of the United States

On 20 January, Ronald Reagan, the Republican candidate, was installed as President of the United States. The three main protagonists (Margaret Thatcher and the Pope being the other two) who forced political change in Europe and presided over the steady collapse of the Soviet Union were now in place. Reagan was a controversial figure, publically proclaiming the Soviet Union an 'Evil Empire' during a speech on 8 March in Florida. (*Tim Graham/Sygma 191 723*)

12 April 1981 – Shuttle

The first launch of the reusable space vehicle known as the Shuttle took place on 12 April. Intended to place payloads in low earth orbit, the Shuttle captured the imagination of the world. It also sparked fears of a new space race, and the Soviet Union considered the system capable (probably rightly so) of deploying weapons in space. During its thirty-year service, two Shuttles were lost, although 133 missions were successful. (*U.S. Air Force photo: Master Sgt. Michael A. Kaplan VIRIN: 050820-F-RZ880-016*)

5 September 1981 – First Camp at Greenham Common

The first semi-permanent peace camp at RAF Greenham Common was established by a group known as 'Women for Life and Earth'. The group, who had walked from Cardiff to the station, typified the fractured nature of the anti-nuclear protest of the late 1970s/early 1980s, as it comprised just women. Subsequently, the peace camp itself became a women-only endeavour, and CND kept its distance.

1981 – Women for Life and Earth

The Peace Camps around RAF Greenham Common soon developed into semi-permanent settlements. Periodic evictions were often brutal affairs and were reported around the world, elevating the camps to the world stage. (*Department of Defence photo DF-ST-84-08474*)

1982 – Falklands Islands War, HMS *Danae*–HMS *Illustrious* Escort

On 2 April, Argentinian Forces invaded the main island of the Falklands. The following day they took the South Sandwich Islands and South Georgia. The islands had been (and still are) long disputed, with Argentina claiming sovereignty. At the time of the invasion, Argentina was under the governance of a right-wing military junta, who gambled (incorrectly) that the British Government would secede the islands.

1982 – Falklands Islands War, HMS *Danae*–HMS *Illustrious* Escort

In an audacious plan, Margaret Thatcher dispatched a task force that retook the main island by 14 June. Thatcher was returned to office, due in part to her belligerent stance with the Argentinians.

12 November 1982 – Yuri Vladimirovich Andropov becomes General Secretary of the Central Committee of the Communist Party of the Soviet Union

Two days after the death of Leonid Brezhnev, Yuri Andropov, former head of the KGB, was installed as the next Soviet leader. He had presided over many of the USSR's more questionable actions, including Hungary and Czechoslovakia and the invasion of Afghanistan. Andropov continued the Soviet trait of misinformation and autocracy. Relationships with the West deteriorating rapidly and it looked like war might come to Central Europe.

1983 – Strategic Defence Initiative (SDI), Star Wars Announced

SDI was the last in a long line of weapons development programmes put into training in the early 1980s. Star Wars was a defence system capable of destroying incoming warheads. The possibility of the Soviet Union developing something similar was, to say the least, remote, but many in the West thought this would push the Soviet forces closer to launching a pre-emptive strike.

30 August 1983 – KAL 007 Shot Down. An SH-2F LAMPS Helicopter Equipped with Magnetic Anomaly Detection Gear Hovers Over the Water as a Soviet Ship Shadows Salvage Operations for Downed Korean Airlines Flight 007

Commercial airliner KAL 007 was shot down by a Soviet fighter aircraft over Sakhalin Island in the Sea of Japan on August 30. All 269 passengers and crew were killed. This event prompted President Reagan to describe the Soviet Union as the 'Evil Empire', with scant regard for human life. (*Department of Defence photograph, Photographer: PH2 Paul Soutar, DN-SN-89-04555*)

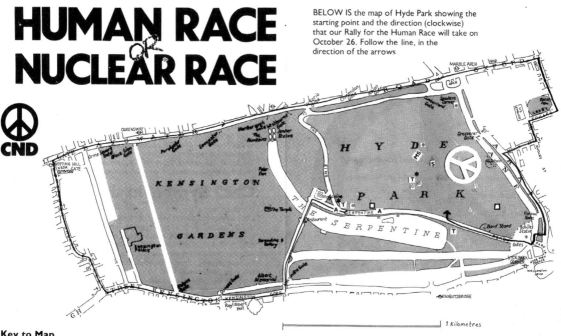

HUMAN RACE or NUCLEAR RACE

CND

BELOW IS the map of Hyde Park showing the starting point and the direction (clockwise) that our Rally for the Human Race will take on October 26. Follow the line, in the direction of the arrows

Key to Map

△ Entry to park after 3.00 pm
⊖ Childrens Area
MS Main Stage
A Assembly Area
S Rally Site

T Toilets
⊕ Skips
⊙ Information Tent
□ Small Platform
★ First Aid
⊕ CND Symbol

If a friend has been arrested

FIRST
● **Stay calm** – Panicking won't help your friend and could cause further arrests.
● Give your friend's **full name** to a STEWARD. Do this when convenient – there is no hurry. People arrested cannot be traced until they have been processed by the Police. This will take at least 1 hour. The Steward will get the name to the HQ Van in Hyde Park. Do not come to the HQ Van yourself as you won't be able to get into the area.
● **Legal Support Unit** – The LSU can only start tracing your friend once we have their full name

NEXT
● **Make notes** – As soon as you can, write down details of your friend's arrest: time and place, friend's name or description, contacts for witnesses (photographers, police officers and nos), your own name, phone no. and address. Date and sign it. This information may be useful for preparing future **court cases**.
● **Pass on note** – Give notes to either a Steward, phone it through to the LSU after the demo on 250 4010 or phone the LSU on Tuesday 29th Oct, between 10 & 6 on 01-388 9689.
● **You! friend!** – Phone the LSU on 250 4010 at least 1 hour after their arrest to find out what's happened to your friend.

The Legal Support Unit

● The LSU will be run by a team of experienced **volunteers** during and after the demonstration. The LSU does not shut down until we feel sure that everyone has either been freed or contacted by us.
● A small team of **solicitors** will be on stand-by, to deal with any problems people have getting **bail**. They will not be able to go to Police Stations personally to give routine legal advice, unless people are being **refused bail**.
● If anyone is **refused bail**, we will do our best to arrange a solicitor for their first **court appearance** on **Monday** to apply for bail. Anyone wanting **legal advice** after the demo should phone us on Tuesday 29 Oct. between 10 & 6 on 01-388 9689. We can give you names of solicitors in London, details of any defendants' meetings and other legal advice.

1 Kilometres

22–26 October 1983 – CND's Largest Protest Yet, London

While the Women's Peace Camp focused on Greenham Common, CND took a more European approach. A continent-wide protest march and rally was organised for October, with an estimated 1 million people attending in Hyde Park alone. The city was brought to a standstill by mass 'die-ins' along the route of the march – symbolically four minutes in duration.

1983 – CND Hyde Park Rally Addressed by Labour Leader Neil Kinnock

Neil Kinnock, the new Labour leader, addressed the rally that culminated in Hyde Park. This was his first major event after winning the ballot. He told the crowd of over 200,000, 'We believe that the only sane use for the Polaris system is to put it into negotiations to ensure our nuclear disarmament and to bring about force reduction in the rest of the world.' It has to be remembered that the majority of nuclear decisions affecting Britain had been made during a Labour government. (*Syndication International – Photo Trends PEO 83-1057-15C*)

Above: 13 February 1984 – Konstantin Tchernenko Becomes General Secretary of the Central Committee of the Communist Party of the Soviet Union

Four days after the death of Yuri Andropov, Konstantin Tchernenko (*second from left, in profile*) was installed as the new Soviet Leader. Andropov was only in the post for fifteen months before dying of kidney failure. It had been hoped the seventy-two-year-old chernenko might last longer, but the plain truth was that the party could not maintain the Soviet system as it currently was – change was on the way. (*Photo: Nova/Sygma 201 949*)

Right: September 1984 – Regional Concerns

The network of Nuclear Free Zones expanded rapidly across the United Kingdom – any Labour authority considered it its duty to oppose the Conservative 'Civil Preparedness' bills wherever possible. A publicity campaign ensued, attempting to win over an apathetic public.

South Yorkshire and **NUCLEAR WAR**

INFORMATION FOR THE PUBLIC IN THE COUNTY OF SOUTH YORKSHIRE

40p

1985 – Local Government Controls, West Wiltshire Control, Bradley Road, Trowbridge

The Conservatives hit back with an ingenious plan. They would offer 100 per cent central government funding to any local authority who wanted new office premises – all they needed to do in return was build a protected control room in the structure. Hundreds took up the offer, although the interpretation of what constituted a protected control room differed enormously. At Bradley Road, a substantial control is hidden under a doctor's surgery in the car park of the council offices.

The Central Control Room at the West Wiltshire Control, Bradley Road, Trowbridge

Forty staff from the local authority, emergency services and military could survive in 'lock-down' for an estimated three weeks here.

11 March 1985: Mikhail Gorbachev Becomes the Final General Secretary of the Central Committee of the Communist Party of the Soviet Union

Just eleven months after being installed as Soviet General Secretary, Konstantin Tchernenko died. The Politburo realised that to challenge the political onslaught from the West a younger man was needed. It came in the form of Mikhail Gorbachev – fifty-four years old at the time of installation – who had some radical ideas as to how to break the arms race stalemate currently wrecking the Soviet Union: Glasnost (openness) and Perestroika (restructuring).

1986 – Operation 'El Dorado Canyon', Libya. Ground Crew Prepares a 48th Tactical Fighter Wing (Lakenheath) F-111F Aircraft for a Retaliatory Air Strike on Libya

The 1986 United States bombing of Libya, code-named Operation El Dorado Canyon, comprised air strikes by the United States against targets in Libya on 15 April, crucially launched from air bases in the United Kingdom. The attack was carried out in response to a bombing of a Berlin discotheque ten days earlier. (*Department of Defence photo. Photographer: Staff Sgt. Woodward VIRIN: DF-ST-88-02676*)

Opposite page: **1986 – Checking Radiation Levels from a Helicopter, Chernobyl**

On 26 April, reactor number 4 at the Chernobyl Nuclear Plant suffered a power surge and subsequent meltdown. A number of steam explosions exposed the reactor core to the atmosphere, resulting in a fire and substantial radioactive fallout being distributed across Europe. Fallout settled across Britain, especially Scotland and North Wales, rendering livestock contaminated. In a vision of what would follow a nuclear war, thousands have since died from radiation related cancers.

8 December 1987 – Intermediate Nuclear Forces Treaty Signed by USSR and United States

After a number of summit meetings between Reagan and Gorbachev (specifically Iceland in November 1985) it seemed likely that nuclear weapon stockpiles might be reduced. Gorbachev offered the complete eradication of his nuclear arsenal by the year 2000, all the United States had to do was stop developing Star Wars systems. This was a step too far for Reagan. The ground was, however, laid for the Intermediate-Range Nuclear Forces Treaty, which was signed in December. All Pershing, Cruise and SS-20s would be destroyed – the pressure had finally been let out of the keg. (*U.S. National Archives and Records Administration NLS-WHPO-A-C44071(15A) 198588*)

Left: **28 May 1987 – Mathias Rust Lands in Red Square**

A nineteen-year-old German pilot, Matias Rust, took his life in his hands, flying a Cessna from Finland to the heart of Moscow, landing in Red Square. The Soviet military tracked the aircraft but did not attempt to bring it down. While a major embarrassment for the USSR, it did allow Gorbachev to remove the majority of those high-ranking officials that opposed his reforms. Rust received a four-year sentence, but only served eleven months before returning to Germany.

Above: 1988 – Final Bunker Phase

It was long recognised that having central government in just one place, be that London or Corsham, was not the best idea, and so a further round of protected structures – this time specifically for the control of the United Kingdom – was planned. Three massive bunkers were constructed at Chilmark (*shown above*), Crowborough and Cultybraggan. All were finished by 1990/91, but were never commissioned.

15–18 May 1989 – Soviet State Visit to China

A four-day summit was held in China with the Soviet Union to open up a new dialogue between the two communist giants. Students, mindful of Gorbachev's requests for reform elsewhere, took the opportunity to mark his visit with a huge protest rally in Tiananmen Square. It was rumoured that Deng Xiaoping would resign; instead, he waited until the Soviet delegation had left and then sent in the tanks. The number of dead remains unquantified; NATO suggests 7,000, but Amnesty International put it at nearer 1,000.

9 November 1989 – *Die Mauer*. East German Police and West German Citizens Watch as a Workman Dismantles a Section of the Berlin Wall at Potsdamer Platz

After a period of increased tension in East Germany, including the army and Stasi refusing to fire on protestors, the Berlin Wall was opened. Only checkpoints were initially dismantled, but within days whole sections were being removed. The reunification of Germany was to take place eleven months later; by then, the euphoria had been replaced with grave misgivings. The economic dream that was West Germany evaporated as it was discovered manufacturing conditions over the border were some of the worst in the world. (*Department of Defense Imagery, Photographer Staff Sgt. F. Lee Corkran, photo no. DF-ST-91-01370*)

21 December 1989 – Romania

Change had been sweeping the European continent since the middle of May 1989 as communist governments fell in quick succession. Surprisingly, most were without major bloodshed; even the East Germans, who had demonstrated a ready willingness to shoot escapees, did nothing. However, in Romania it was to be different. During a public address broadcast live on television, the Romanian President Nicolae Ceausescu was booed and whistled. The secret police eventually opened fire on the crowd, while the army sided with the demonstrators. Four days of fighting ensued. On 25 December 1989, Ceausescu and his wife were executed by firing squad.

1990S

The War on Terror

The monumentous events that swept Central and Eastern Europe over the last two years of the 1980s took Western governments by surprise, although there was no time to claim victory or gloat at the downfall of the 'Evil Empire', as Ronald Reagan once called the Soviet Union. In the Middle East, the collapse of the old world orders increased the bravado of some client governments, none more so than in Iraq. Throughout 1990, Saddam Husain, the Iraqi leader, began ramping up the stakes; accusing Kuwait of stealing oil from wells near the two countries' borders, threatening military action if they did not stop. On 2 August 1990 ,he made good his promise and invaded Kuwait.

Over the next few months, under the banner Operation Desert Shield, countries around the world, recognising the emerging threat to a major energy producing region, assembled a large coalition of troops in neighbouring countries. During the build-up, the United Nations Security Council issued Resolution 678, setting a deadline for the withdrawal of Iraq troops and equipment from Kuwait on or before 15 January 1991. If this did not happen, Iraq faced concerted and overwhelming military action. On 17 January 1991, the crisis moved to a new phase, Operation Desert Storm; for the next thirty-seven days, coalition air forces effectively neutralised the Iraqi defence network. The ground phase of the operation began on the 23 February – it lasted just five days – Saddam's troops were routed.

The rest of the year was dominated by debate as to whether the operation should have invaded Iraq and removed Saddam forcibly. Almost as a sideshow, the Soviet Union had slipped into crisis; politically, financially and structurally. So much so that on 25 December 1991, Gorbachev resigned that evening and the Soviet Flag was lowered at the Kremlin for the last time. On 31 December, the Soviet Union was formally dissolved. No one really noticed; talk was of a new peace and the threat of nuclear warfare pretty much removed. In reality, it was a peace that lasted about a decade before the War on Terror engulfed the world, the consequences of which we are still living with today. And as for Russia, well...

1990 – Iraq Invades Kuwait

On 2 August, Iraqi troops and armour rolled over the border of Kuwait and headed towards the sea. The small Arab state was unable to stop the superior numbers and was quickly overrun. After forty-five years of fearing a Soviet invasion of the world's oil fields, it turned out it would be one of the client states who nearly sparked World War III. Twenty-five years later, the effect of this act of aggression is still with us. Demolished Iraqi vehicles line a roadway in the Euphrates River Valley in the aftermath of Operation Desert Storm. (*Department of Defense Imagery, Photographer Staff Sgt. Dean W. Wagner, photo no. DF-ST-92-09575*)

1991 – Soviet Union Begins to Dissolve

An estimated 500,000 pack Moscow's Manezh Square next to the Kremlin on 10 March, demanding Soviet President Mikhail Gorbachev and his fellow communists give up power. Demonstrations continued on and off all year until some in the party could stand it no longer.

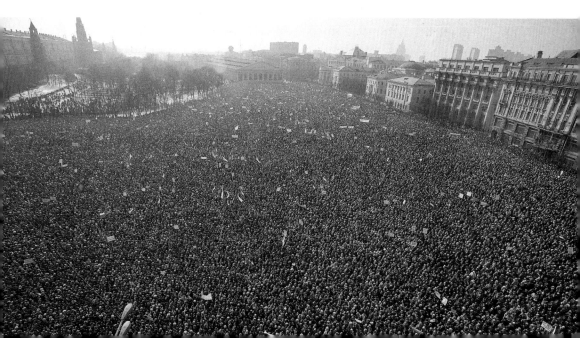

1991 – August Coup, Moscow

In August, while Gorbachev was on holiday on the Black Sea, a group of eight Soviet officials attempted to take power of the Soviet Union. The coup collapsed in two days, but the results were far-reaching. The people, sensing an opportunity to turn their fortunes around, took the initiative and disobeyed the government demands to clear the streets. (*Photograph by David Broad*)

1991 – Boris Yeltsin

The Communist Party effectively collapsed over the next year and a new name was thrust onto the world stage – Boris Yeltsin. He would preside over the collapse of the Soviet Union, its economy and, to a certain extent, its social infrastructure. The West, by then, was too busy to help, looking towards the Middle East and what was to become the war on terror.

2012 – RAF Typhoon Intercepting a Russian Bear-H

A 'battle' traditionally acted out in the 1980s has returned to the northern hemisphere. Fast jets of the Royal Air Force are routinely scrambled to intercept Bears of the Russian Air Force. Meanwhile, Russia's territorial demands in the Ukraine are becoming a real concern to the West. *(Crown Copyright)*